Contents

What is a festival?

A festival is a time when people come together to celebrate.

People celebrate Bonfire Night on the 5th of November.

How Bonfire Night started

A long time ago, some men wanted to kill the king.

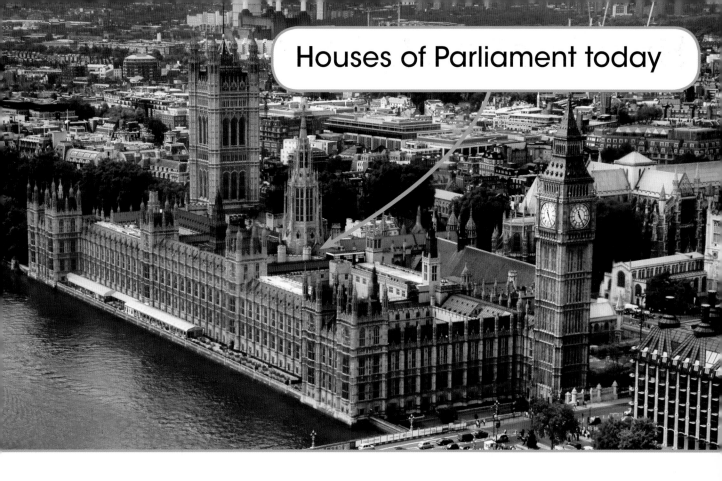

Houses of Parliament today

They put gunpowder under the Houses of Parliament.

7

The guards found the gunpowder just in time.

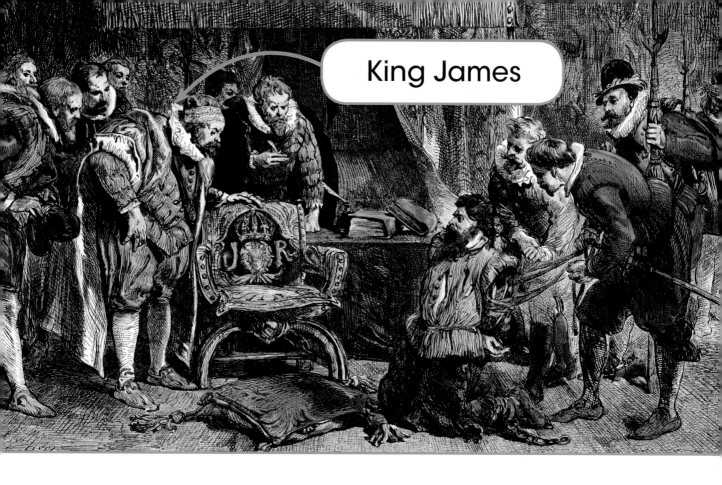

The king was saved.

Guy Fawkes

Guy Fawkes was one of the men who tried to kill the king.

Guy Fawkes

Bonfire Night is also called Guy Fawkes Night.

Celebrating Bonfire Night

guy

Some children make 'guys' for Bonfire Night.

They might ask for "a penny for the guy".

The guys are burnt on bonfires.

bonfire

People watch the bonfires.

People watch fireworks.

The fireworks are very colourful!

Bonfire Night food

jacket potato

Some people cook jacket potatoes in the bonfire.

toffee apple

Some people eat toffee apples on Bonfire Night.

parkin

Some people eat cake called parkin on Bonfire Night.

20

Some people drink hot chocolate on Bonfire Night.

Things to look for

bonfire

fireworks

guy

toffee apple

Have you seen these things? They make people think of Bonfire Night.

Picture glossary

 **bonfire** a large fire that is lit outdoors

 **gunpowder** dangerous powder that can be used to blow things up

 **guy** something made to look like a person. On Bonfire Night, guys are burned on bonfires.

 **Houses of Parliament** large building in London where people who run the country meet to make laws

Index

Notes for parents and teachers

Before reading

Ask the children if they know what holidays and festivals are. Can they name any festivals they celebrate with their families? Can they think of any holidays or festivals where fireworks are used? Tell them that some holidays and festivals celebrate important events in history. Can they think of any historical events we celebrate?

After reading

• Ask the children to think about a time when they have felt that they are not being listened to. How does this make them feel? Explain to the children that Guy Fawkes did not think the King was looking after his people properly. He decided that the only thing to do was to blow up the Houses of Parliament with the King inside.

• Explain that when the gunpowder plot was foiled about 400 years ago (1605) to celebrate bonfires were lit all across England. The practice of celebrating with fireworks began later. Tell the children about the dangers of fire and fireworks. Discuss ways to stay safe on Bonfire Night.

• Show the children how to make a typical Bonfire Night food such as toffee apples or parkin..